"We thank Thee," Rachel prays with grace,
"O God the Cleaver, God the Tiller,
That Thou hast made our anguished race
To be the killed and not the killer."

Cossack Laughter

by

FANIA KRUGER

Dust-Jacket Design by Nione Carson

THE KALEIDOGRAPH PRESS
DALLAS   TEXAS

Copyright, 1937
By THE KALEIDOGRAPH PRESS

SECOND EDITION
June 1, 1938

To *Sam, Aaron* and *Bertha Mae*, bound to me by ties of enduring love and mutual hope for the brotherhood of all men.

Grateful acknowledgment is made to the editors of Household Magazine, Opinion, Holland's, Frontier-Midland, Fantasy, Blue Moon, Dallas Journal, American-Russian Review, Driftwind, Kaleidograph, Better Verse, The Gypsy, The Year Book of The Poetry Society of Texas, Poetry World, Unity (Chicago), Crisis, Choir Practice, American Hebrew, Horizon, Lyric, Voices.

CONTENTS

xi

III.   In Thine Image

COSSACK LAUGHTER

I

SEEDS OF THE SCARLET TREE

Though Hate may rear a gallows high,
Be not afraid, O man, grief-fated:
On the gallows made for Mordecai
Haman was hanged—Truth vindicated.

THE CZAR PASSES

One July noon when I was twelve
  The Czar was coming into town.
(Oh, he will be as bright as God,
  In gilded robe and golden crown!)

I wore my Sunday, cashmere dress
  And lightly ran up Nefsky Street.
My cheeks were flushed, my brow was wet,
  The hot stones burned my naked feet.

The people cheered on every side.
  The hats went up into the air.
Their cry, "He comes, the God of earth!"
  Was half a shout, was half a prayer.

A woman fainted from the heat;
  A child fell, trampled by the throng;
A bearded drunkard clapped his hands,
  Singing a ribald peasant song.

I waited, hoped with quickening breath;
  (The Czar will spread his generous hand,
His word will lift the blight of want,
  And give us freedom, bread and land!)

The Czar will put an end to fear!
  (My heart was beating fast and sang.)
The music sounded, sun gleamed high;
  The anthem played; the bronze bells rang.

He rode, amid the Cossack guard,
  Upon his face death-shadows played;
He came—this puny man in grey . . .
  How can that be? The Czar afraid?

(Why is there need of body guard?
  Why is his face so still and grave?
Why does he cower like a serf?
  The God of Russia is not brave!)

Alone I stumbled up the street.
  My blood ran hot, my pulse beat fast.
All night I tossed in puzzled fear
  After the Czar had passed.

CZARIST CHRISTMAS

The snow has crystalled the window sill
And the howling wind is never still.
The bells are chiming: "Peace on earth,"
But hearts are echoing: "Hunger . . . dearth . . ."

Why do the chiming bells intrude
When the hungry are crying: "Food! Food!"
Unfed, ragged, the sunken-eyed
Irina stoops at her mother's side,
Wrapped in a quilt too thin and old
For warmth against the stinging cold.
Can bells allay the heart's desire
For a loaf of bread and a warming fire?

"Mother, who sings our Christmas song?"
"The nobles, child, well-housed and strong.
The rich who own a tinselled tree
Where candles glitter merrily
Among the spice-cakes, honey-rolled,
And silvered nuts and fish of gold,
While in our hut the spiders spin
Their silver webs in a foodless bin."

"Why are the rich not willing to share
One little cake of the many there?"
"Irina, my child, our Christ is born
Destined to wear a crown of thorn."

Again the bells ring: "Peace on earth,
This is the night of Jesus' birth."

19

The winds, like wolves, are howling low,
Piling in drifts the deepening snow.

"Irina, you're cold.   Why are you still?"
"A light is coming over the hill.
A star, Mother . . . it moves our way;
Jesus of Bethlehem comes to stay.

"I smell the raisined rice and meat;—
Mother of God, now we may eat!"
"Child, it's a vision by hunger fed—
A dream spun out of your fevered head."

"But, Mother, a Christ of love is born;
He bears no cross, no crown of thorn.
He comes like spring; the deepest snow
Thaws wherever his footsteps go.
The grain springs up at his blessed feet,
And he takes the tares from the peasant's wheat.
He will not leave us uncomforted . . .
Mary . . . bring . . . us . . . a . . . loaf . . . of
bread . . ."

Bronze bells ring out their message still:
"Peace and good-will, peace and good-will."

FATHER ON SABBATH EVE

I see my father on a week-day hour,
Exiled and branded, torn with years of plight,
As pale and shrivelled as a frozen flower
Until the candled Sabbath stars his night.
Then, face illumined by his shining soul,
His golden beard combed out to thrice its size,
He straightens like a flame.   So strangely tall
And changed he seems.   I stare in awed surprise.

I hear him pray: "O Sabbath, calm and sweet,
To those who drain the acid cup of woe
You bring a swift release from sharp defeat,
As April flowers are born from frost and snow."
And filled with peace despite pogrom and riot
He blesses one more Sabbath, then is quiet.

ANCIENT HILL

I see my father on an ancient hill
His golden beard is streaming in the sun;
In long *kapota*, he stands straight and still
And lost within Talmudic orison.
I had not seen him for full twenty years
In flesh, and wrapped in *Talis*; tall, revered,
Intoning fervent psalms he stands; the tears
Roll down his cheeks, and glisten in his beard.

What was there on his face and searching eyes?
Glory of dreams, integrity, desire,
Or but reflection of the sunset skies?
Above the Gothic roofs, he seemed a fire!
A shadowy, eternal, sacred flame,
A golden wick within a silver frame!

COSSACK LAUGHTER

Our raftered hut was near a wood
Where, crowned with snow, the dark trees stood

With sheltering arms. When April stirred
The budding flower, the migrant bird,

Proclaiming spring, a cruel wind
Withered the leaf and rudely thinned

The boughs of bloom, while skies turned gray
As pools upon a foggy day.

Life, too, was torn with a gale of grief
Like that which seared the flower and leaf.

That dusk, I, but a girl of ten,
Witnessed the rage of Czarist men.

The Cossacks, who, like winds of hate,
Battered the fence, smashed down the gate,

Shattered the windows, broke the door,
Ripped up the boards of the worn pine floor.

"Death to all Jews!" Their drunken yell
Rang through the hut; our hearts as well.

Father, undaunted with death at his face,
Pled with the Cossacks to leave our place.

A saber's thrust . . . My father's words
Caught as he sank on blood-soaked boards.

My mother cried: "Is God a word,
A broken shield against the sword?"

Only a sudden burst of laughter
From the Cossacks shook the leaning rafter.

With bitter rage, bewildered, wild,
I turned on them, a helpless child,

Trod on their boots that seemed as steel,
Prayed they be crushed beneath my heel.

With lead-tipped knouts they scourged my legs
As they gulped again the vodka dregs.

Our hopes were broken like the chairs;
Blood was clotted on wall and stairs.

Grief-crazed beside the unhinged door
My mother scrubbed the spattered floor.

* * * * * * *

The hut is lost, the czar is gone,
But certain as the dark, the dawn,

Memory of blood upon a rafter
Brings back the ruthless Cossack laughter.

My mother, locked behind a door,
Still scrubs and scrubs a stainless floor.

PILGRIMAGE TO KIEV

Leaving red tracks in the frozen snow,
Wrapped in *pelisses* slowly you go
By day, by night, to atone for sins,
The harvest was ample but bare the bins . . .
While you were entrapped in Czarist snare
Dark lashes cracked through the summer air.
At dusk in the field and back at day's break
When the sun seared your hands at the rake,
When did you, *muzhik*, have time for evil?
Hatred and wrong?   For any upheaval?
You a transgressor?   What sin is yours now?
The earth is abundant by sweat of your brow.

Your breath is labored in cold and sleet,
The ice is biting the rags on your feet.
The snow is up to your shivering knees,
You stagger through storms that blind and freeze.
But onward you trudge that the priests may shrive,
Bound for your Mecca, distant Kiev.

Seven times the cross; you kiss the earth
Who have borne the cross since your day of birth.
Your blood on the field, your blood on the wheat,
While you know hunger, no crust to eat.
The harvest was ample but bare your bin.
Muzhik, muzhik, what was your sin?

SABBATH AFTERNOON

(A village scene in Old Russia)

Within the hut the tea cups clatter
Where kerchiefed women gaily chatter.
Their gushing nipples stop the cry
Of babies. Mothers glorify
This day. They kiss their boys and girls
And pluck the vermin from their curls.
Peaceful they sit, all woes forgotten,
These women dressed in Sabbath cotton.
With sleeping children on their laps
The mothers drowse in restful naps.
Wearied hearts know a brief release
In this weekly legacy of peace.

GHETTO GHOST

Reb Mendel Brodkey in dismay
Chants psalms to take his sins away.

It is Yom Kippur.   Near the ark,
Shoeless, he sways in the candled dark.

Wizened as fruit dried in the sun
Was frail Menucha who had done

The task of two and borne the strife
Like one thrust on the rack of life.

Remembering, his old heart shrinks
In sad recoil, the while he thinks

How tenderly she nursed their brood,
Gathered each day the firewood,

And baked the loaf and knew the plow
While he wore *tefilin* on hand and brow.

While he considered the holy shield,
She drove the cattle toward the field.

He pondered the Talmud's prudent lore;
She peddled goods from door to door.

A comely bride, a wasted ghost,
She was the flower that knew the frost . . .

She was the victim, I the goad
Prodding her down life's stony road.

Candles burn low, the room grows dark;
The letters waver upon the ark.

"Mendel!" He hears an anguished moan.
Is it her voice . . . Or is it his own!

CHAIM

Chaim was a butcher;
It was all that he could do,
For Russia used to limit
The calling of a Jew.

In winter when the moon
Was like a frosty arc,
He rose before the dawn
To stumble through the dark.

With ice upon his beard
He crunched the deepening snow,
The while he chanted psalms
Bitter as his woe.

"Shema Yisroel!"
Compassion gripped his life,
And Chaim grieved each day
That he should wield a knife.

He never tasted meat,
His was a simple fare,
A glass of milk, stale bread,
An apple or a pear.

He watched the ghastly scene
Of meek and waiting cattle
Standing in a row
Like soldiers lined for battle.

To the slaughter house he came
Sorrowing for the slain . . .
Tortured by each blow,
Suffering with each pain:

His heart was pierced when lambs
Uttered a mournful bleat;
But man must live by bread
And ice will cut the feet.

Like sound of ax on wood,
Like sound of steel on stone,
Within his butcher shop
The clash of knife on bone.

Every bloody slash
Made his heart beat faster,
Though killer, he was slave,
The victim was his master.

EASTER IN CZARIST RUSSIA

Katka walks through the village grime:
The April night is icy-clear;
The bells from the jeweled belfry chime
Telling the Easter-tide is near.

She stumbles through the marshy sedge,
Knowing want's clutch and hunger's pain,
To the Cathedral's rambling hedge
Once more to hear the choir's refrain:

"Our Christ has risen life to restore,
Risen to heaven, death is no more."

The candles flame like pointed globes,
Revealing Christ on his golden cross.
The priests are wrapped in silver robes,
And chant: "All save his love is dross."

Waiting the blessing are candled cakes,
Towers of white cheese, eggs tinted red,
 (King of Kings who wept for our sakes!)
Oh, the smell of the Paschal bread!

Katka hears the roar of the wind;
"Forgive, forgive this one who sinned:

"I beg for Paschal eggs and curds,"
Barefoot Katka murmurs low,
"O Lord, forgive these wicked words,
Were You but hungry, You would know."

31

"*Gospodi*, You who are kind and just
Give me a heel of a handled crust!"

With blazing jewels and burnished gold,
Dome and chancel are glorified.
"*Gospodi*, save us from hunger and cold . . .
Oh, the pain in my famished side."

They found her by the willow hedge
When night and shadowy clouds had fled,
Clutching a stalk of frozen sedge,
Brown as the *Kulich*, Paschal bread.

VOLUNTEER

(Russian Revolution, 1905)

"I hear them sing of a worker's shrine,
Of building a world to a new design!

From the Winter Palace, begging bread,
The hungry were driven with lash and lead.
The living are thrust behind prison bars,
Hid from the light of sun and stars.
Beaten and manacled, they must go
To far-off lands of Siberian snow.
Now others are marching.   In one refrain
They sing of passion, hunger and pain,
Of a Czar of hate and the hurricane.
A dirge that burns in the heart and brain.
A song no frost or fear can stem.
Oh, Mother, I am one with them."

*"Whither, my daughter? You shall not go
Where blood has reddened Siberian snow.
The Cossacks will knout you. The knout will smart.
Tanychka, have pity, you break my heart."*

"Banners are waving, the trumpets blare,
Old age and childhood are marching there
Wearing a courage that I should wear,
Singing a song no gale can stem.
Oh, Mother, I am one with them."

"Tanychka, pity me. Do not go!
The sun will set. Sharp winds will blow.
In a night too dark for stars to shine
The Cossacks kill, oh daughter mine."

"I would rather die in a core of flame
Than wear a coward's robe of shame.
A freshened wind is blowing wide,
No one can stay the rising tide.
I hear the voice from a worker's shrine,
Building the world to a new design!
Though feet be frozen, and backs be red
With mangled flesh, from even the dead
I hear the call, I hear the song,
I hear the song no sword can stem,
And I go to join the marching throng,
Oh, Mother, I am one with them!"

SEEDS OF THE SCARLET TREE

(Russian Revolution, 1917)

While hungry hearts of Russia weep,
Oversurfeited, the landlords sleep.

Blind to death's shadow on the wall,
Blind to the menacing hidden leer,
The landlords feast in the banquet hall
But what of hearts broken with fear?

Too long like russet autumn leaves
You toiled while others gleaned the sheaves.
Now you who know the wind, the frost,
Arise from life's dark holocaust.

"Why are we beaten?" voices cry,
"Though one with the earth, why are we fed
The stones of our seeds, a husk of corn,
A mildewed crust in place of bread?"

The hungry march.   Red banners wave
Like ships borne on by a flaming sail,
Within their hearts a tortured song
Accompanying the icy gale:

"From serfdom to the days of hope,
Released from bondage of the past,
We shall create a life for all;
The overlord's day is waning fast."

(Once children lost among the weeds
They sprouted from the fallen seeds!)

The harvest sown by rebel lives,
How thick upon the autumn field
Your wall of slain and nameless dead!
What will the crimson harvest yield?

EPITAPH FOR A MUZHIK

You know the sting of lash, its cruel pain
And cringe before the thong as once again
It falls upon your flesh, you see your home
A squalid hovel, and the fallow loam
You once laboriously kept plowed and tilled
And full of growing grain, now filled
With refuse. Upon this hardened earth
Your dripping sweat, the price of life from birth
Till death should come. The narrow dusky lane
Of life made sodden by oppression's reign.
To royalty you gave luxurious food
That you and yours might starve in plenitude.
Your labor and your sweat made rich the ground.
Bewildered now, you hear a trumpet sound,
A loud clear peal of freedom, *muzhik*, hear!
The dawn is come, no more the air of fear.
Soaked to the bone, you rise from swampy grave
To warmth beneath the free sun of the brave.

DEATH OF GORKI

You were the blossom on spring's thorny vine,
The wind, the rain, magnificent and free.
Though you had tasted sorrow's flood of brine,
Your spirit burned like sunlight on a tree,
And sublimated by your life and art
The lower depths, the broken-down in heart.

Ever our minds perceived you not of flesh,
We live the hours of days gone starkly by—
You were the grace of sunlight's golden mesh,
The strength of wind, the blue arc of the sky.
You have not died whose toilsome dreams have spun
From dismal dark the luminous rays of sun.

II

AMERICAN GHETTO

When we have opened wide the darkened gate,
Gleaning the harvest of sky and earth,
Then we shall love and, loving, turn from hate
And know exalted freedom of rebirth.

REB BERREL IN AMERICA

Always for another day,
Reb Berrel puts his dreams away!
Hour after hour his needle creeps
Moth-like until the twilight sweeps
Day from the sky. He sings a song
To keep his heart-flame bright and strong,
A song of how, with autumn's leaf,
Shall come the ending of his grief,
A song of how he yearns to bring
His bride from Russia in the spring.

Reb Berrel, once so tall and slim,
Is labor-bent and worn and grim;
He sews within a shabby store
As chill winds penetrate the floor,
Sodden with rain and dungeon-damp,
His only fire a crooked lamp.

He mends old coats with tireless thread
For coins to buy salt fish and bread.
Each Friday night he leaves his store,
Barring the ancient clumsy door
And goes to *Shul*. He knows the pain
Of aches that come with wind and rain,
And prays for courage. Day by day
He toils and puts his coins away.
The day Reb Berrel spent his gold
(Looking not quite so bent and old)
To get a ticket that would bring
His eager bride to him in spring,

A letter came with foreign mark.
He read it once, his face went dark:
"The burning drought, the dreadful blight,
Has turned our sunny land to night;
Rachel Friedman, your famished bride,
Was sick two weeks. Last night she died!"

Reb Berrel, once so tall and slim,
Is labor-bent, and worn and grim;
He sews within a shabby store
As chill winds penetrate the floor,
Sodden with rain and dungeon-damp,
His only fire a crooked lamp.
Always, for another day,
Reb Berrel puts his dreams away.

CANDLES IN A CROCK OF SAND

(Eve of the Day of Atonement)

While death is drumming the window sill,
A Jewish grandam, bent and ill,
Reads from her prayer book. Close at hand,
Candles burn in a crock of sand.

She plaited the wicks at the rise of the sun;
Her moulding of candles and prayers was one,
Then she set them aflame for daughter, for son——
"A gleam for the living, a light for the dead,"
She moans as she nods her kerchiefed head.

Hallowed by twilight, mellowed by faith,
In a broken voice and frail as a wraith,
She pleads with God: "O Thou unseen,
Pass me not by, but make me clean."

She hears *Kol Nidre,* an exile strain,
Its music heavy with ancient pain.
With eternal sadness deep in her eyes
She beats her breast and, praying, cries:

"O give us peace, reveal Thy light,
Our Lord of love, our God of might!
And be forgiving, O my soul,
To those who hate, and pay hate's toll."

Searching the darkening autumn sky,
She sees her passing years go by.

She visions Moses on the height of a land
With a flaming torch in his sacred hand
That lights the wick in the crock of sand:

A light for the living, a prayer for the dead;
A flame for youth and the hoary head,
A beacon light for the clown, the sage,
And a shrine of love for the coming age.

Aware of death on the window sill,
A tired woman, bent and ill,
Prays solemnly, while near at hand
Candles burn in a crock of sand.

MARRIAGE WIG

What is that goading Sara's heart
   Sharp as a scimitar?
A Hebrew bride must wear a wig.
   Such the customs are.

Her glossy hair, a silken crown,
   And all the charm thereof,
Is this the price that she must pay
   For husband and for love?

Somewhere a thrush begins to sing,
   Then fall her weeping words:
"O man enslaved, O man enchained,
   Learn freedom from the birds!"

Within the bridal room she hears
   The slow and shuffling feet
Of the wigged crone whose dangling shears
   Must make the law complete.

The scissors snip, the dark hair falls,
   No lock has been denied;
What though her heart be torn with grief?
   The law is satisfied.

The marriage wig is on her head,
   Tradition played its part;
Though April buds are burgeoning,
   Winter is in her heart.

OLD ALREADY

Oi, oi, my daughter," mournfully deep
My mother cries: "You make me weep;
Oi, marry Jacob, Joseph or Moses,
I will give you silver, buy you roses.
I see no husband, no feast is spread,
No marriage wig upon your head.

"I am aged and bent; the shadows creep,
And soon my hands must fold in sleep.
Oi, marry, my daughter, the sun grows dimmer,
The moon is losing her magic glimmer;
Your days of youth are all but done,
You are old already.   You are twenty-one!"

JEWISH GRANDMOTHER

In the darkened room a figure sways.
(Upon the wall a shadow plays.)

A grandmother with a furrowed face,
In soft black dress and cap of lace,

Is gazing down an unseen aisle
Where prophets march in ghostly file.

Passover now—triumphant day!
Freedom is born and she must pray.

While a thousand legends vex her mind
She hums the songs of a life maligned:

Drought has consumed the deepest root,
Blizzards blighted the early fruit;

Brutal songs of Pharaoh and death,
The scorching puff of a Cossack's breath,

The moldy cave wherein to hide
When spurs of Cossacks clanked outside;

Of broken boards where her husband lay
And the mound of earth that covered his clay.

In the darkened room where shadows fall,
She is not there—not there at all.

* * * * * * *

She sits in her rocking chair, alone,
Chanting in rhythmic monotone.

Merged with time, she sits in her chair,
Darkness over her face, her hair.

One with the ticking of the clock
. . . Rock . . . rock . . . rock . . . rock . . .

GHETTO PASSOVER

The autumn leaves are washed away
By winter rain.
This spring Passover eve,
With sharp refrain,

Young Jacob speaks: "Wherefore this night
Of solemn feast
And ancient customs we observe
Brought from the East?

"Long years ago in Egypt land
Of cruelty
God led us forth from hate and greed
And slavery.

"We feasted ere the exodus
From that old land,
Our loins were girded . . . our staff
Within our hand.

"And as we broke unleavened bread
Waiting the morn,
An angel slew with flaming sword
Egypt's first-born."

"But, father, that was long ago
We slowly marched
Toward Canaan's land . . . Our hearts are starved;
Our throats are parched."

"The soul of peace will sing once more
And make life just and fair.
Son, we shall mount the hill again
From out this new despair."

"Weary, bewildered, now bereft
Of bread, of freedom's light,
Afraid and desolate we live.
Wherefore this night?"

"Shadow and hurt will disappear
As rain is done.
The time of singing now is come,
Jacob, my son.

"Let courage be your shield, your sword,
Faith's unquenched spark . . .
Go forth and bravely meet the dawn
That lifts the dark."

The saintly father chants and peers
Through dusk and chill;
The young moon shines upon his son,
Mounting the hill.

NAOMI DANCES A KAZATSKA

In the ghetto of America; in the ghetto of this alien
 land,
Naomi dances a Kazatska, a mad, mad dance.
The ache in Naomi's heart loosens itself to her limit-
 less joy.
Drinking her wine of glory from a hollow cup
As no king has ever drunk,
She dances to a realization of a dream:
Her daughter's marriage.

Naomi's daughter has skin smooth as old ivory,
Her hair is as dark as the wind at dusk,
Her eyes as soft as the moon.
Naomi's daughter has been schooled in the school of
 America.
The young man she marries
Knows only the ghetto of America and the school of
 America.
They watch Naomi as she capers up the aisle before
 them.

Down and up—up and down—dances Naomi,
A humped bent figure dancing without restraint;
While her hands clap, while her hands beat,
She moves her faltering feet.

And as she dances, with each waft of the wind
The flaming candles, fragile as herself, dance with
 her.

Puffing as an erratic wind, faltering...stumbling...
A braided *sheitul* trembling on her head,
Naomi whirls on, before the bride and groom
As they leave the altar of the synagogue.

In a tremulous voice she chants and cheers:
"O joy be with you, bridegroom and bride!
O bliss be with you!"

Who, looking on, can know
That Naomi dances the last wave of hope,
Her daughter's marriage;
That she dances away the undertone of her grief,
The overtone of her life,
That the rhythm of the Kazatska looses the merciless
    weight of years
Which lay against her heart like a crushing stone,
That Naomi dances away from the life of Czarist
    Russia:
Famine, pogroms, black hate;
The lashing of Cossacks' knotted whips,
Stinging like winter winds through naked woods,
The bleeding wound, the bruises, the scars,
The fears at dawn, the nights without stars,
The violent deaths of her loved ones,
The massacre of her husband, the prayer of dying
    lips . . . . .

Murmurs . . . whispers . . . chuckles . . .
Who, looking on, can guess
That Naomi trembles from terror and starvation,

That her feet are withered from walking naked in
    the Russian snow?
Who can explain why her lips
Are drained of blood?
Her soul shrivelled like a dry reed?
Her body scarred from Cossack whips?
How her heart suffered wound after wound, until it
    is numb to pain?

Her shuddering body cannot long endure
The rhythmic movements of the wild dance.
Her trembling hands clap out the accompaniment
To her frost-bitten feet.
She claps her hands and dances,
Crying out: "Thank God, I lived to marry off my
    child!"

Down and up she dances,
Up and down.

The watchers laugh . . . whisper . . . chuckle . . .
Heads turn away to escape dust kicked by her faltering
    feet.

The veiled bride blushes;
The groom frowns.

YOSEL

He hears their cry at dawn,
It haunts him in his sleep:
The quick and anxious wail
Of oxen, calves and sheep.

This is his task: to kill—
To know the anguished pain,
That man may fare on meat
Though fields blow free with grain.

Serenely munching grass,
Are cattle in the shade,
Drinking from argent pools,
Fearing no whetted blade.

And when these cattle fall
Into the blood-stained dust,
Yosel, in his own heart,
Can feel the *chalif's* thrust.

When meadows, plains and trees
Afford abundant food,
Why kill the lamb, the calf?
Why must the knife draw blood?

BARUCH THE SHOEMAKER

"Nu, what shall I say? Oi, I ask of you,
Is there no place for an old, old Jew?"

Bitter of heart, in the dusk of a cellar,
Baruch, the shoemaker, hammer in hand,
Laments his plight, a lonely dweller
In a world that cannot understand.
The tumult, the shouting of changing news,
What do they mean to a mender of shoes?

His beard falls over the wrinkled leather
As he taps and taps, bewailing his grief
That is lost on the world like a wind-blown feather,
Or a brittle and broken autumn leaf.

"Oi, why must one dwell unloved, alone
With a barren heart, as cold as stone?"

What shall he say, who knows but toiling
From dawn till dark with a gnawing breast,
Tears for his drink, and the sharp pains coiling
About his limbs . . . As the sun goes west.
He is a candle burnt to the core,
An ancient house with a crumbling floor.

Bitter of heart, in the dark of a cellar,
Baruch, the shoemaker, hammer in hand
Laments his plight, a lonely dweller
In a world that cannot understand . . .

"Nu, wherefore my life? Oi, I ask of you,
Has the world no place for an old, old Jew?"

WHOM THE NEW MOON MOCKS

The sky unfolds a starry cover
Above the April leaf and lover.
　　Alike young love, a diadem,
　　Touches Sinai and Bethlehem.
Youth sees the charm of bud, while age
Perceives the fruit and heritage
That clings to weathered foliage.
　　But love defeats theologies
　　And creeds of men and deities.

Old grandam Rachel built a fence
Of love against malevolence,
　　Lest evil touch her orphaned lad:
　　Her daily task to make him glad.
She rocked him in the Talmud law
That he might learn and live in awe
　　Of God; and like a Sabbath flame
　　A holiness enshrine his name.
Thus Rachel prayed her Joseph be
As rain on parchéd land, free
　　Of all that baffles like a fog—
　　A gold light in the synagogue.

Frail in the flesh—in will a giant—
From Rachel's lips curses defiant
　　Fall on her grandson if he stray
　　From the ancient Hebrew prophets' way,
Or wed with one not sheltered in
The fold of faith.　"If this his sin

And should he dare to flout belief.
Let life for him be dark and brief.
O hear this prayer! that pain devour
His day as frost consumes the flower."

Like flesh and bone, like fowl and feather
Her prayer and curse have grown together.
   While curses fall, light deifies
   A thin new moon in clear blue skies,
A moon that mocks her futile words
As transient as the flight of birds.

And what of Joseph, who had wed
A gentile bride? Love comforted
   And made him happy for a space,
   Giving to the world a Springtime face.
But who may know when Death will creep
Intent on silence, intent on sleep?
   A boisterous wind and blinding rain
   Muted the rumblings of the train
And death swift dropped from out the dark
To kill joy's quick tumultuous spark.
   O hour when eager life is caught
   And crushed beneath a juggernaut.

Now darker than the dusk of death,
Grief stays the warmth of Rachel's breath,
   And grips her throat with claws of steel,
   Until, immune, she does not feel
The cruel wind, the icy weather;
Her prayer and curse have grown together.

Oh, who is there can stand defiant
Before young love and death, the giant?
Like a stricken tree where crows carouse,
Or like a long deserted house
  With eyes two clouded moons she stares
  At peaceful stars. Too deep her cares,
Too stark her grief—This was her plan:
To rear in faith, to train a man
  In Hebrew law to be content
  To go the way the prophets went.
And he who dies, his faith betrayed
Must bear the name of renegade.

The new moon mocks her pious grief;
He went as goes an autumn leaf,
  For love defeats theologies,
  The man-made laws and deities.
And spread against the dark of night
A cabalistic script of white
For love's enduring anchorite.
  The sky unfolds a starry cover
  Above the young leaf and the lover.

BURNED BREAD

(Hebrew Tradition)

As an offering to God, with my hand I throw
Into the fire this bit of dough.
As it burns and the flames arise
We shall gain a paradise.

"Grandmother, will you never tire
Of burning bread in the flaming fire?"

"Hadassa, why do you question so,
Begrudging Fate its mite of dough?"

"So little for food, and yet each day
You are casting the precious dough away."

"We dower our God who will send us gold
The way the Holy Book foretold."

"And sweets and bread?   We daily go
Hungry and faltering through the snow."

"God will make warm the wintry wind
Till wine flows from the Tamarind.

"The trees will bear great loaves of bread,
The ice be melted, the hungry fed."

"Then, Grandmother, burn the dough and pray
That God send this gracious gift today."

As an offering to God, with my hand I throw
Into the fire this bit of dough.
As it burns, the flames arise,
Wafting prayers to paradise.

WORDS BEFORE SLUMBER

"*Ach,* son, truth in the Talmud's pages
Reveals when the Messiah appears,
Spring will subdue the winter rages,
Peace drive out war and ruthless fears.
Sleep, orphaned one, and I will sing
Of our Redeemer."

                Bright grows the face
Against her breast. The sleigh bells ring
Through narrow lanes where snow lies deep.
Wizened as poverty itself,
The grandam chants and shadows creep
Like hands of a clock upon a shelf.

". . . And the Messiah, the revered,
Will come into a quiet room
Where a scholar with a silver beard
Is reading in the purple gloom.
The early dawn will bring anew
The bud of promise, the day of rest,
Your mother watches, waits for you
Where starry truths are manifest.
The miracles again be told:
Red wine will flow from the tamarind,
The trees will shine in blooms of gold
And stillness tame the noisy wind.
No more shall want or famine dare
Start through the land from North to South,
But luscious fruits on boughs once bare

Will satisfy each craving mouth.
Ach, then, the old may claim new birth.
The bread, like fruit, will crown the tree,
The children's songs will rule the earth,
And slaves and prisoned men be free."

The tale has lulled the child to rest.
He dreams upon a silver stair—
His mother holds him to her breast
And chants a universal prayer:
The dream of dreams!   No grief, no weeping;
The world in beauty, joy remade.
While grandam naps, the child is sleeping,
Exalted, smiling—unafraid!

III

IN THINE IMAGE

We whisper futile fears to walls of stone:
"Life's day is dark." Even when white drifts cling
To hill and field, in quiet undertone
The bulb and seed wait patiently for spring.

UPWARD

In my own image I bore you, my son—
A slave to earth.

So in my youth I spoke,
So in my youth I reproached myself
For having given birth.

Since then hail has beaten upon my head,
Sorrow has covered my flesh,
Winds have swept my soul,
I have drunk from tuns of torture
And tasted drops of triumph,
Reaching for the goal.
Then I, my son's measuring line,
The base for his flight, kept towering.

Now as a bird before the winter flight,
Now as a bee with his honey gathered,
I watch this child in the deep vastness of the air,
Though tossed and weathered,
Gallantly braving the wind, passionately flying.

In the sky, light and shadow interchange
To seem like one.
My child will know not only bits of shadow
But immensities of sun.
He will taste not only drops of torture
But drink great cups of triumph.

You are stronger than I have ever been, and braver;
You have passed beyond the measuring line
Of depth and height . . .
Reach upward . . . upward.
O son of mine!

FOR A CHILD

I brought you, my child, into this world of rough-
    ened waters.
My heart is torn with conflict of this earth.
I would hold you tenderly and let the thorns pierce
    my flesh
That you shall have no after-throe of a sting,
I would chant to you of blossoming vines
And never once reveal that flowers fade.
I would gather the fruit and taste it first to know
That it is ripe and good for you to eat.
I would let you walk in ignorance
Beneath the sheltering dark,
Then I should have done all within my power.

But I know:
You could not walk complacently *alone*, when skies
    are dark.
Your body would have no bruises, yet it would
    know no healing.
You would not fall; yet would not know the rise
    from falling.
You would eat the gathered fruit, yet not know
    the joy
Of pulling apples from the loaded tree.
The residue of fire cannot know the blaze of life.

With courage for comrade, through the dark,
You must clear the rocks of this imperfect earth
And find the peak and have the will to go.

Then my spirit shall rise even at the darkest twilight
Be with you, watch over you,
And hold a lantern above the waters of your sea
Until morning returns again with the strength of
    understanding.

RIVER OF MEMORIES

Where the blue waters of the Neva
Break on the shore in ageless play,
I, with my older sister, Olga,
Sought fluted shells one summer day.

I watched cloud argosies go by
With pallid sails flung to the wind;
Her gleaning eyes saw but the sand,
And how small grains were disciplined.

Because my hand was swift to find
The pearly shells on love's highway
She envied me my vivid dreams,
Because her own were vague and gray.

What if we quarreled that vanished hour?
Since then the tides of hate have run,
And stormy grief has followed us,
To blot that distant springtime sun.

Since then we felt the knout, the blade,
And knew life's darker, grosser ills,
We saw young blossoms crushed in dew,
We saw how years have levelled hills.

Our measured days so soon must cease,
Now, Olga, let me press your hand.
Calm, in the twilight hour of life
All hate is done.   I understand.

Forgotten are the shells and pebbles,
Lost with the ocean's windy roar,
Washed by the restless, flowing river,
Gone, to return to us no more.

Now, walking by the river Neva
In memory, shadows growing long,
I, and my grey-haired sister, Olga,
Hark to the water's broken song.

PATTERNED BY PAIN

Lying in pain as shadows darken the window,
I glimpse the moon, a thin, silver horse-shoe,
And stars in a field of grey.
How white the clouds between the stars and the moon
Like a waterfall, tumbling!

I turn and turn
Through the darkness,
I fumble the sheet in my hands,
Unable to find rest or sleep.
I hear the groans of other sufferers,
Footfalls of nurses,
In this house of pain.
The moan of agony begins to spread
Throughout the world.

Moments . . . hours
Still the pain,
While death, who hovers near, makes the slow de-
cision
To whom he shall give peace.
Then—at last—an hour's ease from agony
And out of the darkness
A voice:

From grey designs of pain, from webs of sorrow,
The spirit weaves the raiment of strength.

WELL DOES HE KNOW

Three times, in austere secrecy,
Death came in pale disguise.
He must be starkly bored with me
Because I did not rise
And follow him.
                        Well does he know,
Like dusk pursuing day,
He will return, and I will go
The unfamiliar way!

IRON HANDS

One said, "Now we have made each wheel
Like cunning fingers formed of steel
To slave for us, to set us free
Of servitude and drudgery
That we might know, like weed and flower,
The joy of sun and springtime shower."

Another answered: "Without toil,
Can there be harvest from the soil?
And, without labor, who will give
The needed bread by which men live?
For though the hands of steel may hold
For a chosen few its coins of gold,
What of those whose toil is past
Since iron fingers work so fast?
Machines can prove a Frankenstein,
Instead of blessing, curse malign,
And give man's hunger but a crust
And grind his body into dust.
Better the iron hands grow numb,
Go back to earth they were taken from,
Unless such fingers formed of steel
Toil for joy of the commonweal."

OVERNIGHT OIL TOWN

When steel and oil and gold are master,
Life gleans but anguish and disaster.

*   *   *   *   *   *   *

Where fields and fruitful orchards stood,
The land lies fallow in the sun,
Save for the towers of steel and wood,
Derricks, each like a skeleton.

With noise of derricks overhead,
(She who could one time pitch the hay)
The widow Anne creeps out of bed,
Slave to the stark routine of the day.

Each night within this Texas town
Of chugging wells, of flaming gas,
Crazed by her grief, slow-witted, brown,
She asks the laborers who pass:

"Where is my Johnnie, my small son
Who went to work with his water pail?"
(He was her last and only one,
Her smiling lad, freckled and frail.)

"When will my little son be back?"
One driller stops: "He's a comin' soon."
Anne stumbles to her ruined shack,
Humming a simple nursery tune.

"My boy be comin' home again."
She smooths the quilt on his narrow bed.
(Her Johnnie sleeps in the sun and rain
With a stone for a pillow at his head.)

Her boy who took his father's place,
And died when the flaming oil went wild.
(They never showed her his blackened face;
He was her last and only child.)

"Old crazy Anne," the drillers say;
Breathing instead of the spicy blooms
Of flowers and fruit, and the yellow hay,
The smoky oil and the gassy fumes.

There is no time for petalled springs
Where man through lustful circumstance
Struggles for gold and stubbornly clings
To the ancient game of Midas' chance.

Against the smoky skies are seen
Only the derricks, far and wide,
The meadow lands and the fields once green
For these were blighted, rotted and died.

* * * * * * * *

When oil and steel and gold are master,
Life gleans but anguish and disaster.

SEAMSTRESS

The lamplight silvers her greying hair
As she sews a garment she never will wear.
Stiff as her needle, and pale as the seam,
She stitches and binds a vanished dream.
Shadows creep through the dusty door,
Where scraps from her scissors litter the floor.

At dusk, head bent, and too tired to rest,
She makes of Fancy a welcome guest.
The spools of her unwinding thread
Are haloes cast around her head.
Weary with toiling, she falls asleep,
The folds of garments seem waves of the deep.
Then, waking once more and back in her chair,
She sews a gown she never will wear.

SAINT MIHIEL, MARNE AND PICARDY

"One, two and three, one, two and three.
This is the toll war took of me . . . . ."

The mother croons a grim refrain
To the cry of wind, to the tap of rain;
For her heart is bare as an autumn field
Bereft of the fruit of its splendid yield:
"One, two and three," her plaint runs on,
"My David, Paul and Jonathan,
My three tall boys forever gone."

At the Marne her David cursed the war:
"Damn it . . . . what am I dying for?"
In the thick of fighting Jonathan fell
And Paul was gassed in Saint Mihiel.

Night does not bring forgetful sleep,
Nor can she quietly sit and weep,
Whose grief is like a sharpened goad
That prods her on the murky road,
Chanting, unheard, the grim refrain,
To the cry of wind, to the tap of rain:

"One, two and three, my life, my all,
My David, Jonathan and Paul,
This was the toll war took of me,
One, two and three, one, two and three,
Saint Mihiel, the Marne and Picardy."

PARADOX

Strange, is it not, old men at ease
Are plotting war at greed's desire,
While it is always youth who sees
The clash of steel, the withering fire.

A CRY FOR BREAD

A cry for bread is a futile cry
When a million starve and a million die,
When a million die and a million freeze
That one may have his unearned ease.

Death and hunger—hunger—death—
God, what a price to pay for breath!

IN THINE IMAGE

(A Negro Speaks)

What color is Thy face, Lord,
Black as mine?

When I turn from black to brown,
From brown to yellow,
From yellow to white,
Wilt Thou change, too, Lord?

Art Thou a black God?
Or art Thou a brown God?
Art Thou a yellow God?
Or art Thou a red God?
When the sun softens into the moon,
When the moon glimmers into the sun,
When the day darkens into the night,
When the night wakens into the day,
Dost Thou change, too, Lord?

What color is Thy face?
Black as mine?

In Thine own image, Thou hast made me, Lord.

UNLIKE THE SWAN

Unmastered sorrow yields the heart
No hour of spring;
Unlike the swan, the daunted die
Before they sing.

RESURGAM

A blade from out the dark earth breaks,
And then the jonquil's sudden gleam;
A leaping miracle that makes
Both saint and wanton dream.

TREE PHILOSOPHY

The trees have their own strategem
At filling space alloted them,
And should not men's philosophies
Be wise as all sagacious trees?

CHALLENGE

Your flowering generation too has known
Exile and wounds and tears . . . Reclaim your own!
Go onward, son; I shall not bid you stay.
A braver *I* is born in you each day.

DEEP SOWING

O aching heart, transcend and fortify
Your hurt with lyric words, by tender sowing,
Till you can voice, above life's troubled cry
The raptured wisdom of eternal growing.

MY SOUL A STAR

My body is a supple cedar
Proud winds may twist, or bend and break;
My soul, a star firm fixed and shining,
No wind may touch, no storm may shake.

DREAMER'S MEADOW

He toils and dreams
   In every weather;
Life and the dream
   He plows together.

And slow or swift
   In the soil of sorrow,
He plants a song
   For the new tomorrow.

And fields that know
   His tender keeping,
Are lashed by storms,
   Prelude to reaping.

But what to the dreamer
   Is squally weather
When the dream and the crop
   Have grown together?

MESSIAH

Has the Messiah come?
Or is He the ever-coming?
Racing with clouds, a light against shadow,
Or as the sun turning the night into dawn,
To be lost again in darkness?

What is a Messiah?
A word of peace to scatter the gloom of war?
Youth, with its dreams and yearning,
Flowering into manhood,
To old age, and then once more into youth?

Is he a child conceived in love?
A wave upon the widening sea?
A star at twilight?
The struggle, the groping and climbing to the crest
    of a hill?
The oak from the acorn?
Life from death?

Has the Messiah come?
Or is He the ever-hoped for, the ever-coming?

If each of us be but a blade of grass,
And touching one another, O comrade cherish
Each neighboring blade, and let not hate enflame
Life's field, or blade by blade, we perish.